G000069138

For a good colla Sorohón

Christian

May 1998

The Serial Books Architecture & Urbanism series results from discussions held between Duncan McCorquodale, Nicholas Boyarsky and Nicola Murphy in late 1996. During the course of these talks we recognised the need for a forum wherein issues concerning contemporary architecture and urbanism be debated in as broad and accessible a way as possible. It is with this promise that the Architecture & Urbanism series is published.

Boyarsky Murphy's Action Research, appropriately the first title in this series, will be followed by the work of, amongst others, Kevin Rhowbotham, Michael Hensel and Tom Verebes (.O.C.E.A.N UK architecture and urbanism), and Raoul Bunschoten/CHORA.

The Serial Books Architecture & Urbanism series is kindly supported by the Alvin Boyarsky Memorial Trust.

SERIAL BOOKS
Architecture & Urbanism 1

Action Research

Boyarsky + Murphy

Contents

As students at the Architectural Association during the mid-eighties we witnessed the conclusion of a range of experiments that had been initiated in the previous decade. This period engendered a new formalism that embraced the complexities suggested by new technology. Process, an art technique from the seventies, offered an informal but increasingly personal alternative.

Neither route could answer our questions about how to simplify the making of architecture so that it can actively engage in the changing present. This publication illustrates a working method developed over the last few years in response to a number of critical contemporary issues: the re-emergence of housing as a priority, the growing predominance of periphery over centre and the urgency of large scale urban issues. To achieve a fluid and heuristic approach to the present condition calls for critical redefinition beyond modernity. The architecture of postmodernity has consistently looked beyond itself to art, science, history, technology and philosophy. Supermodernity offers the excesses and the overabundance of events of the present as our source. While this loss of control offers possibilities for unlimited excess it also presents the opportunity for reaction, for the establishment of new fundamentals.

Action Research developed from this paradox. We began to discover that simple everyday actions (to throw, to cut, to stack, or to layer, for example) could generate coincidental models capable of responding to the complexities of architectural production. Moreover the logic of each action could accommodate chance and the accidental. Procedures of action, observation and further action then led to moments of crossover: questions of appropriation, decisions about scale, the weight of matter and the politics of a situation.

At an urban scale rules and structures to sustain dynamic growth are brought into play. This process is contrary to techniques of automatism where the presumed loss of authorship can result in the replacement of one formal structure with another. It is informal in the sense that there is no hierarchy, no weighting of value on any particular moment.

The consequences of any action are at the same time infinite and limited and controlled by the nature of the action itself. An action exhausts itself by generating a range of secondary infinitives...

The Hague

Erasmus Zone

Urbane Landscape

The Randstad, the area between Amsterdam, The Hague and Rotterdam,

presents a model of a highly ordered yet amorphous landscape of expanding cities. The potential of this condition suggests a dynamic

Scatter Plan
Wateringse Veld, The Hague

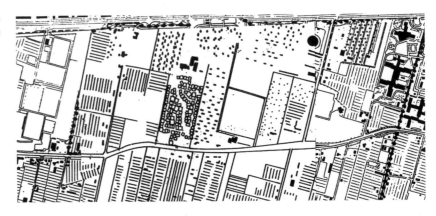

field of negotiation and change that is organic and flexible — a laboratory for research and experimentation. The challenge of activating this landscape offers new opportunities for re-evaluating housing and planning.

Housing has traditionally concerned itself with containment of the masses. To be housed is a passive act of submission. Sameness is reinforced by the multiplication and repetition of basic units within fixed frameworks. To inhabit, on the other hand, is to take an active part in one's environment. It is to introduce diversity and choice. To plan is to think ahead, to account for all eventualities, to control over time. Planning thus concerns itself with what it can know (zoning, infrastructure and transport systems) rather than the unknown or the unquantifiable. The technocratic ideal of controlled, phased development rules out the accidental and the creative mess of every day life. It embraces historical precedent as a distraction from formal and programmatic invention.

To recognise that one idea, or set of principles, cannot sustain a project is to admit a loss of control. To loose control shifts a predetermined process into game playing. To play is to re-invent, to assume new roles, write new narratives, to enter the mythic world of foundation. Play operates beyond conventional time. If urbanity, a rich mix of density, disjunction and programmatic layering, is achieved over time, the simulation of these qualities can only be successful by the incorporation of chance and the accidental. The current massive housing programme in Holland would appear to jeopardise this dynamic balance by a huge injection of normative matter. There are inevitable social, economic and political factors behind this. Yet the lost opportunity can also be attributed to the reluctance of architects to question precedence critically and in so doing enter an open ended future. The early modernist concept of Siedlung, for example, invokes the notion of settlement in or colonisation of unknown, virgin territories. In this missionary work rational, ordered models can be superimposed onto a razed surface. The endeavour depends on a position of moral certainty, a denial of any pre-existing qualities and an overriding sense of being in control. To continue practicing this method, without belief, is to pay lip service to a bureaucratic inheritance.

The Erasmus zone, situated just beyond the 1950s edge of The Hague, has been earmarked for development as a themed Georgian-style parkland. In its present state irrigated fields are covered by disused greenhouses that now provide winter parking bays for thousands of caravans. To settle this landscape with housing units sets in motion the inevitable procedures of land clearance, road layout, orientation, distribution of plots and construction. To break or agitate this process at any stage opens up a number of variables that alter any predetermined outcome. As a consequence of this action the plan is liberated.

One hundred and fifty housing plots of mixed social groups were scattered over the site in a number of 'throws'. The random nature of this action allowed models of density and variation to emerge that could not be achieved by the overlaying of a single system. After these actions the throws were refined by the insertion of primary roads, parkland and secondary roads, causing further densification and disjunction amongst the plots.

Throw

Plots

Scatter

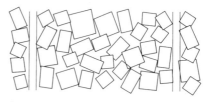

Primary roads

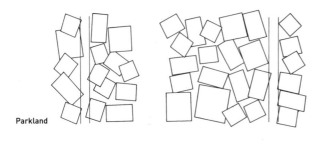

Parkland

Twist

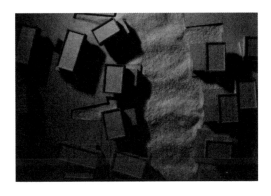

This first move opened up new possibilities for public and communal space, circulation and landscape. In the process of shifting plots a number of internal, trapped spaces and semi-private circulation routes evolved. The existing canal system was then reintroduced, partly buried in culverts, exposed in parkland and running through trapped spaces and circulation routes which became small communal wetland ecological areas. Other trapped spaces became shared wild gardens. Public and vehicular circulation adapted to the residual spaces between plots and landscape.

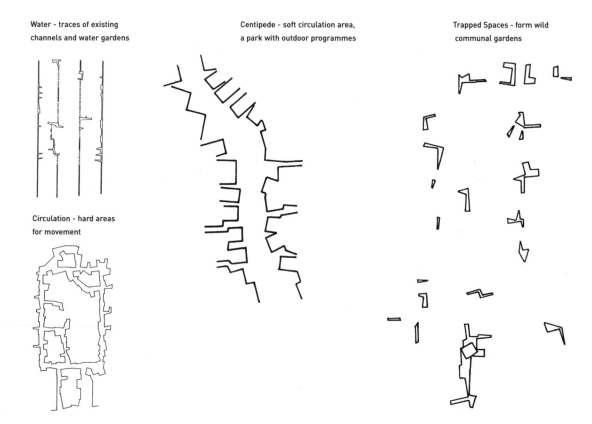

Water - traces of existing
channels and water gardens

Centipede - soft circulation area,
a park with outdoor programmes

Trapped Spaces - form wild
communal gardens

Circulation - hard areas
for movement

Houses of all categories are divided into two distinct layers. The ground floor, generally situated orthoganally within each plot, comprises living, kitchen and dining areas. Openings are controlled both to ensure privacy and to extend living areas beyond the plot, borrowing neighbouring walls, trapped gardens and parklands.

The separation of the two levels allows the upper floor to shift and rotate independently to maximise privacy and orientation to the sun. This shifting begins to form local configurations and aerial courtyards. To allow for shifts and rotations between floors the stairwell becomes a void which extends beyond the imprint of the ground floor.

Shifting Plots - plan detail

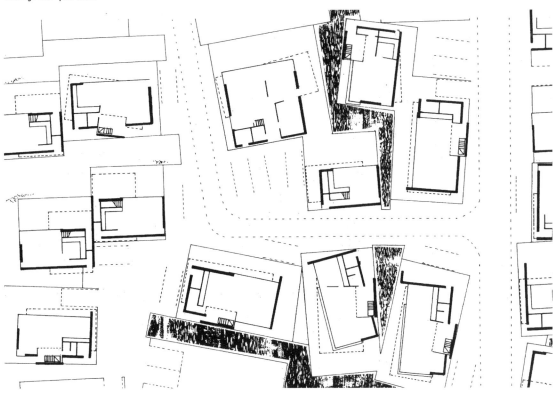

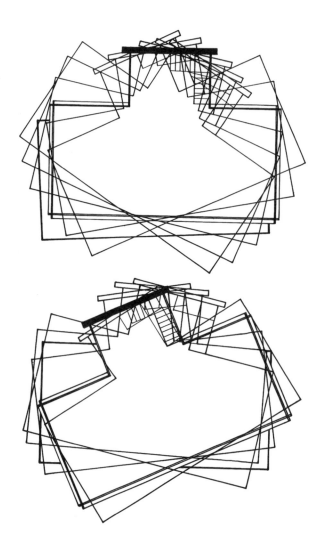

Insalubrious Island No. 11

Zac des Amandiers

Menilmontant

Paris

North of the Père Lachaise cemetery, in Paris' XXième arrondissement, Menilmontant has been in existence since the Middle Ages. It was primarily a fruit growing area and over time the espaliered orchard boundaries became formalised into party walls. By the middle of the nineteenth century it comprised very dense narrow plots with shops, workshops and cafes at street level, speculative housing above and deep courtyards with a second layer of houses and workshops. The district, was declared insalubrious in 1900 becoming Ilot 11. Ilots, predominantly in Eastern Paris, represented areas where mortality from tuberculosis was three or four times higher than in wealthier districts. Marked for rebuilding, Ilots were abandoned to slow decay. In the case of Menilmontant no further action was taken for almost seventy years. Ilots inevitably attracted waves of immigrants and while living conditions resembled some of the worst slums in Europe a rich social mix developed.

This freedom from bureaucratic control allowed strong local identities to flourish. By 1995 the majority of Ilot 11 had been demolished and the narrow plots amalgamated into large postmodern housing projects. Many of the original inhabitants, despite promises to be rehoused, had been evicted by the developer. Some sixty original buildings remained amongst swathes of rubble.

Zac de Amandiers, Menilmontant

Menilmontant formed part of the Goose Game project organised by Claire Robinson who commissioned a number of French and international architects to prepare alternative schemes to this ongoing process of total erasure. In response to the developer's strategy of tabula rasa, local resistance urged a policy of restoration and rehabilitation. The Goose Game reinforced this by co-ordinating a proposal for refurbishment and piecemeal infilling with new housing units.

The history of Paris from Haussmann and Le Corbusier to Matta-Clark reveals moments when the process of demolition has suggested qualities and possibilities that could transform the city beyond the limitations of conventional architecture and urbanism. However both the totalising vision of the ZAC's developers and the holistic instincts of the resistance shared a sense of closure. By proposing fixed solutions the fate of the ZAC was sealed. This project took the possibilities of demolition and a landscape of abandonment as its premise to actualise the historic city.

ZAC des Amandiers

1974
The Concerted Development Zone (ZAC) des Amandiers is determined.

1995
The majority of the ZAC has been demolished, the project is scheduled for completion in 1997.

1900
Declared Insalubrious.

1953
Master plan drawn up.

1975
The city of Paris gives the project to Semea XV development company. Their brief is to rehouse 4,300 inhabitants within 5 years.

Haussmann's strategic beautification of Paris relied on the clarity of axial planning and on the logic of single point perspective. This ordering could only be achieved, however, through an intimate understanding of the complexities of medieval Paris. In 1853 Haussmann ordered the preparation of an accurate map of Paris. All over Paris scaffolding towers were erected with platforms higher than the surrounding rooftops from which surveyors triangulated the entire city.

We began by projecting lines across the site that broke with existing geometries of street and party wall. These lines mapped new relationships. They became cuts in the fabric that tied together existing activities, suggested new and unexpected combinations, and allowed for new insertions. Cutting through the void of an abandoned lot, through the solid of a building and the void of its interior, we began to describe a new spatiality. The cuts took on two different characteristics. Penetrating lines opened up, formed connections and allowed for insertion. Lines of reflection disrupted, distorted and rotated existing configurations.

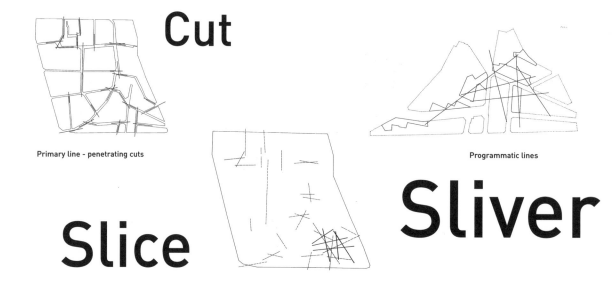

Cut

Primary line - penetrating cuts

Programmatic lines

Slice

Sliver

Secondary line - reflecting cuts

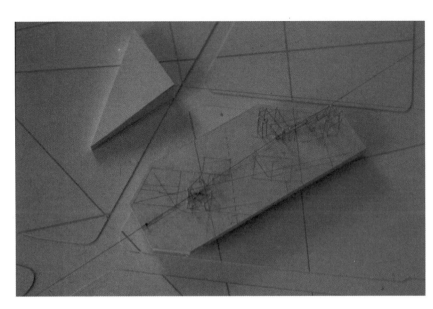

Cutting model

Reflecting Lines

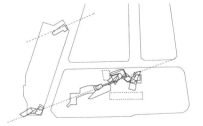

Production Lines

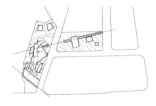

Ground condition and leisure lines

Georges Haussmann
In his Arcades project Walter Benjamin described Haussmann as an 'artist of demolition'.
Howard Saalman has written of 'the kind of conceptual simplification' which resulted in
'the transformation of small-scale complexity into monumental simplicity'.

Walter Benjamin
'For him the political choice was not between historically preserving Paris
and modernizing it, but between destruction of the historical record — which
alone makes revolutionary consciousness possible — and destruction in
remembrance of this record. In short it was a choice between obliterating
the past, or actualizing it.' (Susan Buck-Morss)

Notes on Demolition

Le Corbusier
'Surgery must be applied at the city's centre. Physic must
be used elsewhere. We must use the knife to cope with that
evolution which has passed through so many stages and
has turned the ancient Lutetia into the Paris of today.' 1927.
In his scheme for Ilot insalubre no. 6 of 1936, Le Corbusier
proposed its total replacement with greenery, slabs and
point building. This ubiquitous urbanism surfaced in the
1953 proposal for ZAC des Amandiers.

Gordon Matta-Clark
'These buildings were among the last standing in the plan of
modernising the Les Halles-Plateau Beaubourg district.
The work was interesting as a non-monumental counterpart
to the grandiose bridge-like skeleton of the Centre just behind.
For two plaster-dusty weeks people watched us measuring,
cutting and removing the debris from the truncated conical void.
The base of the cone was a circle of four metres in diameter
through the north wall. The central axis made an approximately
forty-five degree angle with the street below. As the cone
diminished in circumference, it twisted up through walls, floors
and out the attic roof of the adjoining house. This hollow form
became a Son et Lumiere for passers-by or an extravagant new
standard in sun and air for lodgers.' Conical Intersect, 1975

Guy Debord
'... with a careful rearrangement of fire-
escapes, and the creation of walkways where
needed, open the roofs of Paris for strolling ...
slipping by night into houses undergoing
demolition, hitchhiking nonstop and without
destinstination through Paris during a
transportation strike in the name of adding
to the confusion, wandering in subterranean
catacombs forbidden to the public.'

Once the pentrating lines had been cut they began to attract programmes that fed off existing activities and their traces. They introduced mobility across the site. Activities could expand and contract over time borrowing found spaces and culturing their own forms. Four programmatic categories were proposed: commerce, production, leisure and institutional.

Refract

Reflect

Penetrate

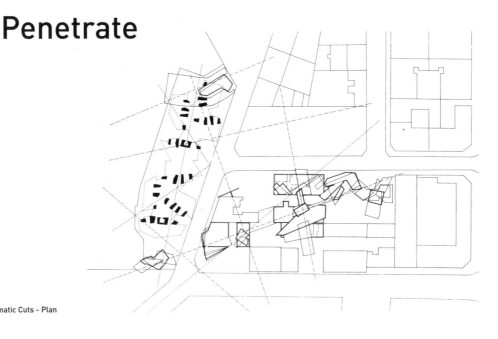

Programmatic Cuts - Plan

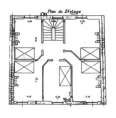

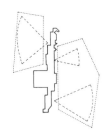

19th century speculative housing,
25 rue des Partants

Walls attract and sustain
living clusters

Against the Grain

The walls of Menilmontant exert
a narrow political influence on
an insecure and shifting ground.
Perpendicular to the street pattern they reinforce
Haussmann's two-dimensional concept of elevation
as scenographic backdrop.

Traces of party walls rotate and reconfigure

Dwellings cluster

The land surveyors' mark persists, precluding
fundamental new approachs to housing and the
urban field despite changes in landownership.
When exposed through demolition these party walls form new elevations of
matter that reveal traces of interior division, crude servicing and a monolithic
idea of gravity. Our strategy of cutting against the remaining grain created
routes and sections that led to the introduction of new programmes,
the development of degrees of institutional complexity
and the suggestion of an anthropological landscape.
To inhabit and to house this landscape meant operating
on the walls themselves. Lines of reflection generated
a new action list: to rotate, to break, to fragment,
to project, to suspend, to realign, to reconfigure.

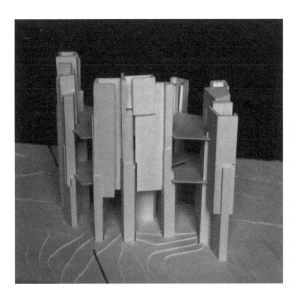
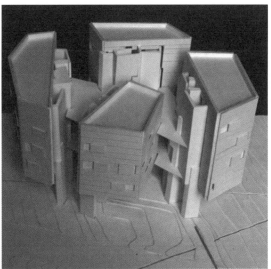

Cluster Housing - section

Programmatic Model

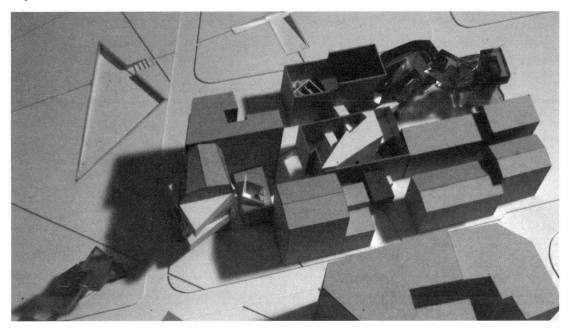

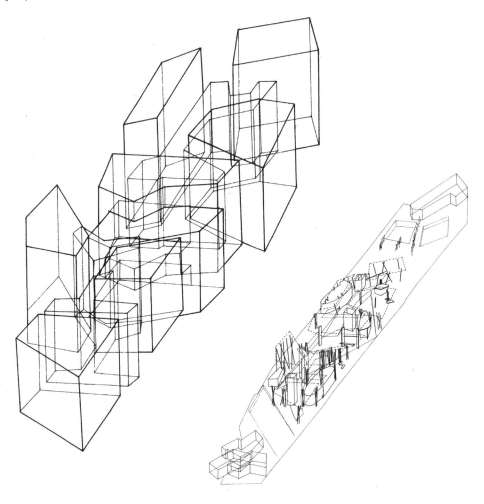

Clusters

The rotated traces of the party walls provide footings for new inhabited supports. As these cast walls grow vertically they mutate from structure to programme enabling shells of inhabitation to cluster and be sustained. The interface between the historic city, the actualised landscape and interior experience is constantly negotiated and redefined by movement around, through and inside the walls.

Cluster Housing – interior view

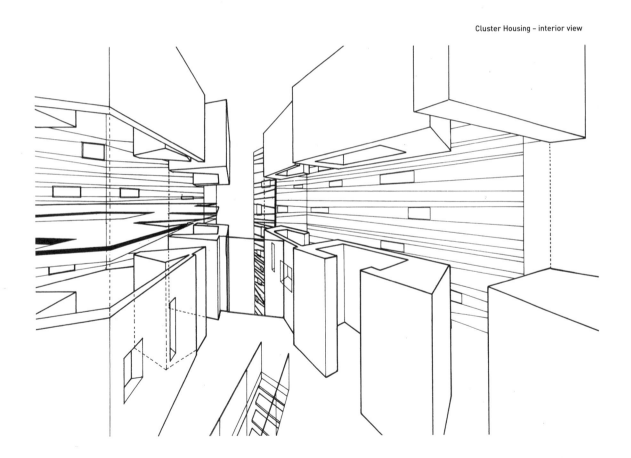

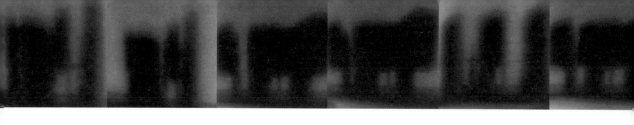

Cluster Housing Prototype

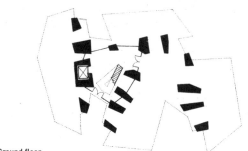

Ground floor

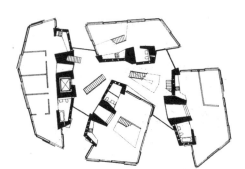

First floor

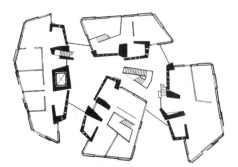

Second floor

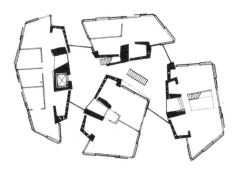

Third floor

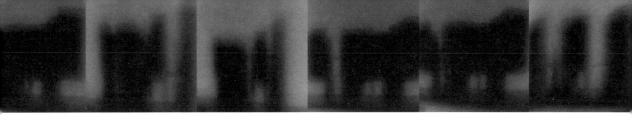

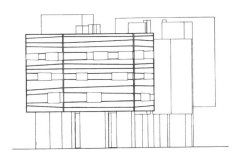

East elevation

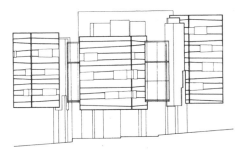

South elevation

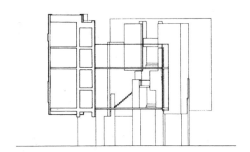

Cross section

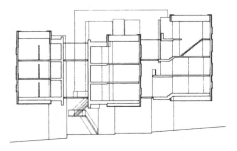

Long section

Seoul

National Museum of Korea

South Korea

Tongjak Bridge flyover, Seoul

On the Road

A national museum to
'achieve the globalization
of Korean culture' and anticipate
the unification of North and South Korea.
The prospect of overheating Far Eastern economies
and a contemporary lack of cultural identity provided
an intriguing scenario for action. The brief revealed
a nostalgia for the postmodern museum, suggesting
a marooned colossus in arcadia.

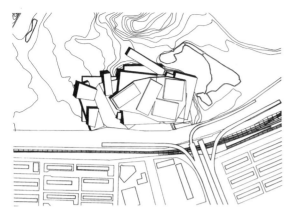

Site plan

Model

The incomplete nature of the collection,
a collage of ancient Chinese, Japanese and
Korean artifacts and artworks suggested
a container park of goods in transit.

The site, a former US army golf course and heliport on
the Sobinggo highway, is a flood plane at the base of
the foothills of Mount Namsan. This naturalistic backdrop
crashes into a disjunctive urban landscape of highway,
railway lines, the unfinished flyovers of Tongjak Bridge,
and an immense slab city stretching down to the Han River.

The simple action of stacking individual layers of programme and testing them against gravity opened up a secondary verb list of procedures. Hand actions were then scaled to the site. Elements such as the the plate and the pool were brought in to structure and contain the stacked boxes. The details, or critical moments, of this landscape of speed, orientation and object are defined by the gaps, voids and accidents of cross-layering.

Plate

Stack

Pool – upper gallery

Shift

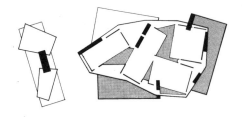

Adminitration level

Shuffle

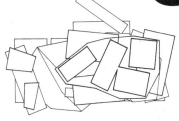

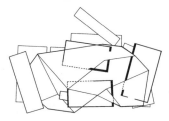

Composite plan

Main gallery level

Cut through upper galleries

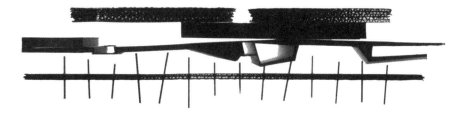

Cut through plate and main galleries

Cut through composite model

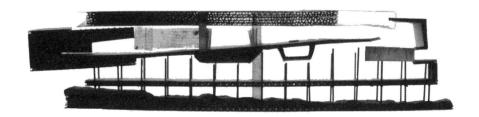

Over

Into

Pool over gallery

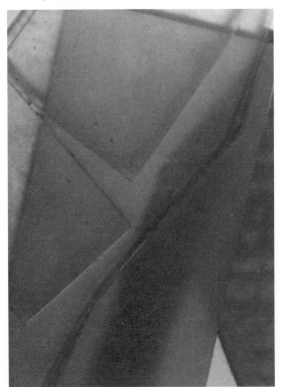

Gallery entry from plate level

Pool cuts through gallery at high level

Through

Consequencial Detail

The detail has always been endowed with a certain moral value. There is, however, according to his biographer Franz Schulze, no record that Mies van der Rohe ever uttered the aphorism 'God is in the detail'. The phrase was coined by Gustave Flaubert in a totally different context and surfaced in 1955 in the introduction to Erwin Panofsky's 'Meaning in the Visual Arts'.

  This misattribution has conveniently masked a panoply of professional insecurities and long been the cause of both an almost pathological myopia and a riot of fetishistic speculation.

Detail has traditionally been a question of materials, of matter meeting matter. The realisation of any project being ultimately resolved by the achievement of the standard detail. By some curious economy of scale, the larger the building the fewer details. However, if construction details do not make architecture but only ungodly buildings where does one look?

Architecture's moral repressions surface again in the strict categorisation of the components of design: programme and event do not, for example, appear in construction drawings. Time, void or chance encounter are never detailed. Wilhelm Worringer, writing at the beginning of this century on the origins of abstraction, highlighted this dilemma when he spoke of 'man's immense spiritual dread of space'. This fear, a residue from a period of human development when man was not yet able to trust entirely to visual impressions, substitutes touch and the easily recognisable for the unknown.

In working through the museum project by stacking, shifting, layering, sliding, twisting (a world of infinitives), it became clear that incidents and coincidences initiated change and development. These moments revealed ambiguities. When something fitted there was no means of progressing. A misfit, on the other hand, opened up new possibilities. These interruptions and inconsitencies became residual within the project. The detail was in the action.

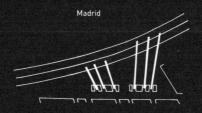

Madrid

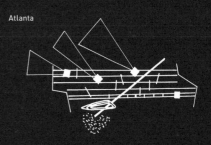

Atlanta

Urban Actions

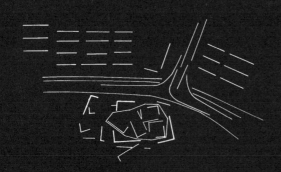

Seoul

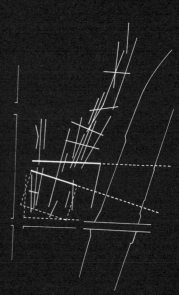

Melbourne

The Hague

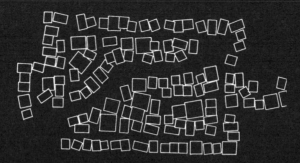

Euston

Paris

Thessaloniki

There is an elemental
aspect to the periphery.

URBAN ACTIONS

Things just happen. Parasitical growths
around motorways. Illegal housing beyond
the tracks. Industrial abandonment.
Large sheds. All seemingly random releases of pressure
from the centre. How to operate within this field? The urban
consequences of Action Research imply a shift from an architecture that
is expressive of the forces within the city to one that structures procedures
for actualising the city's fabric. In other words letting things happen.

Osmosis provides a model to understand forces at work. It allows for unrelated elements
to coexist as projections and collisions of differing origins. This projectile urbanism accepts the
existing city as found. There is no geometry, rather an understanding of pressure and its release
either directly or sublimated through the urban membrane. Osmosis suggests certain procedures.
Intensity can be transplanted from one situation to another. Zones of indeterminacy can allow for
the unexpected. Collisions can be engineered to hit or miss.

Pavlos Melos
Aerial view of former barrack

The West Arc Thessaloniki

The western edge of Thessaloniki comprises empty army barracks, abandoned tobacco warehouses and illegal housing sandwiched between sea and mountain. To colonise these voids and integrate them within this fabric called for a structuring device that could intensify the existing dynamics of the area, accommodate inevitable patterns of growth and introduce a range of new activities and material conditions. A metaphor for this structuring can be found in osmosis.

Three broad edge conditions were identified: hard, porous and indeterminate. Each edge forms a membrane that allows elements to pass through or to be caught within. These elements can change the profile of the edge itself. The hard edge, comprising nineteenth century-style solid square blocks, implodes programme into each site. Voids and empty lots from the irregular, industrial blocks of the porous edge, are implanted into the empty barracks to form sports and leisure fields. The indeterminate edge comprises areas of uncontrolled growth. The membrane registers this energy. Landscaped strips control the incursion of elements. Elsewhere concentrated points of inserted programme begin to influence the surrounding areas. Informal programmatic areas occur throughout the site as direct osmotic pressure points. Landscape becomes critical void: the space between conflicting elements; intense moments of outdoor pleasure and new topographies of osmotic pressures.

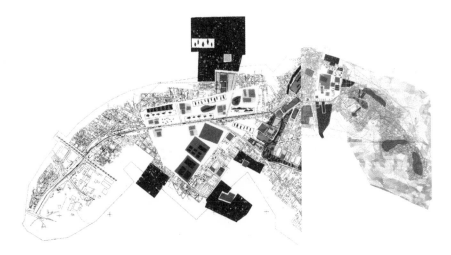

Site plan

Osmotic conditions

a) Abandoned voids
b) Imploding programmatic point
c) Lodged programmatic point
d) Landscape membrane
e) Lodged housing
f) Informal programmatic point
g) Absorbed programme
h) Exploding programmatic point

Porous edge

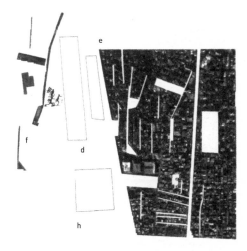

Indeterminate edge

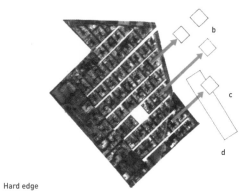

Hard edge

Euston

Railway Projects
The railway, on the otherhand, is deeply embedded in the nineteenth century city. Redundant land and disused tracks describe a condition of pure entropy. The artificiality of these levelled lands and their loss of economic and social primacy provides the basis for further layerings and new connections. The projects for London and Melbourne describe two approaches. At Euston a vocabulary of new landforms was developed that could accommodate a range of new programmes. At Melbourne the decked over tracks formed an osmotic membrane that could react and respond to the historic urban context while generating new landscapes and connections.

Highway and Railway Projects

Highway Projects
The highway has a distinctive yet atopian presence. The horizon of atopia, as Michael Newman has written, is not infinite but indefinite, combining movement with inertia. The aura of this generic landscape of both speed and congestion holds itself apart from any context. To broach this state of autism is to unleash raw undirected energy. The projects for Atlanta, Madrid, and Seoul suggest different approaches. In Atlanta the mediated, interior experience of the car and highway is intensified in a web of virtual devices that connect car to office to hotel room to street, appropriating sound and image, repeating and rescaling into a condition of spectacle. In Madrid the crash, the random, disjunctive and eroticised chain of events, provides the means for transplanting velocity and its physical attributes into domestic life on the periphery. In Seoul high culture meets roadside in stacked containers.

Double Overpass, Atlanta

The void above the Interstate is laid with suspension cables that stretch from North to South. These cables support a shifting landscape of liquid display units and large panels of lenses that both magnify tall buildings to drivers and reflect sunlight into the shadowy canyons. The cables respond to heat and movement, shifting constantly. A bridge stabilises the cables. Video cameras are positioned on the Interstate, at street level and inside buildings. Images are relayed throughout the site, interrupting hotel TVs and appearing on large screens. Radio antennae on the double overpass interrupt programmes. Tall buildings become the backdrop for major night time projections. A large cloud, depending on the time of year, will either rain or steam providing relief for the TV Park below.

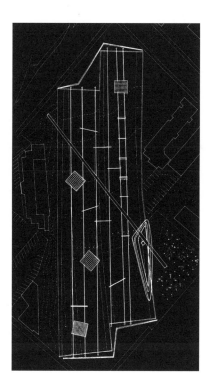

M-3, Madrid

Implanting elements of the highway into surrounding neighbourhoods opens up
a new vocabulary. The motorway's edges, the berms, barriers and verges that
currently form a hard edge to the periphery, become the membrane through
which aspects of speed, collision and moving matter can pass. In this case regular
housing blocks are cut by radial lines of vision from moving cars. The voids formed
by these cuts disrupt the blocks providing entry points and breaks through to the
city behind. They begin to bend and distort the plan creating domestic accidents:
entry hall collides with kitchen, crashes into bedroom, collapses into bathroom
and crumbles into balcony.

Motorway as landform

Crashed floor plan - model

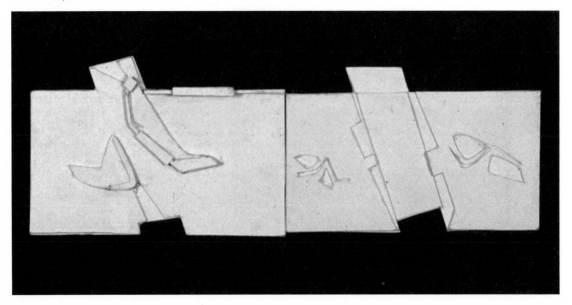

Federation Square, Melbourne

Decking over the railway lines between Melbourne's business district and the Yarra River, Federation Square's Wintergarden forms a membrane between the city and its riverside. It attracts, filters and projects, connecting to the nearby sports precinct with lines of activity, courtyard gardens and programmatic landscapes. These lines project through the Wintergarden disrupting the Swanston Street axis with an informally structured square that expands and contracts according to different events. The Wintergarden atrium's elevation shifts diagonally in response to these pressures. It implies a larger civic square that brings together St Paul's, Flinders Street Station and the Concert Hall. This move creates a void within the city for interior landscapes.

Landscapes model

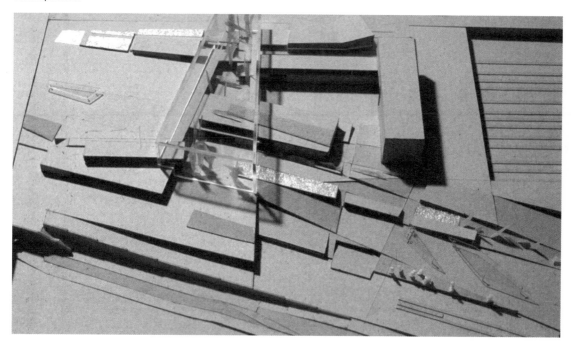

The West Arc, Thessaloniki
Jason Coleman, Stacy Nokano
and Eiffel Wong

Double Overpass, Atlanta
Structural Engineers
Michael Baigent and Orla Kelly

Federation Square, Melbourne
Jason Coleman and Silvia Ullmayer
Model
Jason Coleman

Acknowledgments

Erasmus Zone, The Hague
Jason Coleman
Landscape Consultant
Annie Guilfoyle
Model
Jason Coleman
Greenhouse photograph
Susanne Isa
Photographic study
Laure Thorel

Menilmontant, Paris
Peng Ghee Tan and
Jason Coleman
Models
Peng Ghee Tan and
Jason Coleman
Photographic study
Laure Thorel

National Museum, Seoul
Jason Coleman and
Beat Fleischli
Structural Engineers
Michael Baigent
and Orla Kelly
Model
Jason Coleman
Photographic study
Laure Thorel

The authors would like to
thank Victoria Boyarsky
for her help and support,
Laure Thorel for her
photographic collaborations,
and, for his support and
comment, David Greene.

All rights reserved. No part of this publication may be
reproduced, stored in a retrieval system, or transmitted,
in any form or by any means, electronic, mechanical,
photocopying, recording, or otherwise, without the prior
permission of the publisher.

ISBN 1 901033 45 7

Colophon

All opinions expressed in material contained within this publication are those
of the authors and not necessarily those of the editor or publisher.

© 1998 Black Dog Publishing Limited and the authors
Edited and produced by Duncan McCorquodale
Designed by christan@chkdesign.demon.co.uk
Printed in the European Union

British Library Cataloguing-in-Publication Data.
A catalogue record for this book is available from
The British Library.
Library of Congress Cataloguing-in-Publication Data:
Serial Books 1, Architecture and Urbanism – Action Research.